Bow's Notes

K.W. Bow

Copyright 2016 by Kenneth W. Bow
The book author retains sole copyright to
his contributions to this book.
Published 2016.
Printed in the United States of America.

All rights reserved.

No portion of this book may be reproduced, stored in a retrieval system, or transmitted in any form or by any means – electronic, mechanical, photocopy, recording, scanning, or other – except for brief quotations in critical reviews or articles, without the prior written permission of the author.

ISBN 978-1-9860028-4-7

Front cover design by Mark Gauthier.

This book was published by BookCrafters,
Parker, Colorado.
bookcrafterscolorado@gmail.com

This book may be ordered from
www.bookcrafters.net and other online bookstores.

Foreword

Thank you reader, for selecting my book. There are many choices of books and we all have a limited window of time to read. I appreciate you purchasing my product. It is a humbling thing to know someone would choose to purchase, and then read your work. I do not take it as a small matter. By purchasing and reading a book, the reader and the author form a certain bond as they travel a road together for a short time. It is especially rewarding when the two agree on the content. It is my hope you can find inspiration and life challenges in the pages of this small booklet.

From the days of my high school years I have found the Bible fascinating. I have travelled to Israel on two occasions to learn more about the land and culture of the Bible. I worked on an archaeological dig and lived on a Kibbutz to better inform myself of how to understand this book from God. I have read it from cover to cover over twenty times, and it is still as exciting to me as it ever was.

The Bible is a magnificent journey and experience. It is ever a delight. In it you will travel to distant lands and meet some of the most incredible people of history.

It will introduce you to kings and peasants. You will walk the palace halls of castles and the open fields of the countryside. You will meet the famous and be introduced to people whose name we will never know. You will read some of the greatest love stories ever told and you will see the dark side of man as the evil manifests itself in heinous ways. Every emotion of man is highlighted at some time. You will see greed and avarice and murderous covetousness. You will also see the greatest examples of love and sacrifice that mankind has ever contributed. For indeed the Bible is the story of man. It is the whole story, and nothing is left out or omitted. It is the ultimate mirror of life.

When we invest time in the Bible we indulge a bit of the eternal. The Bible will never pass away, even in the eons of the future. If you have read it sincerely then my hope is this small work will intensify your understanding and enjoyment a little more. It is the grandest journey we can make while in this life. Thank you for sharing a portion of your life journey with me.

Kenneth Bow

Table of Contents

Introduction..1
Ten Commandments...3
The Prophets..7
Major Prophets..9
Minor Prophets..13
The Monarchy...18
Judges..22
Psalms...27
Song of Solomon..32
Isaiah...36
Jeremiah..40
Ezekiel..45
Daniel...48
Inter-testament Period..53
The Talmud..59
Jesus...63
Matthew..74
Mark...78
Luke...80
John..83
Acts..86

Introduction

Welcome fellow Bible student. By purchasing this book I realize you have a desire to know more about the best-selling book of all time. So if this is your first foray into Bible study or if you have worn out many Bibles along your journey, Welcome.

I would imagine while most of us were in high school and college we became aware of a small booklet called Cliff's notes. Little yellow booklets that were condensed overviews of books and other things. The purpose of these notes was (and still is), to save you time and give you a basic thumbnail version of the subject matter.

My purpose is the same. I am hoping to save preachers' and saints' time in their quest for Bible knowledge and understanding. These are versions of my studies and thoughts. My conclusions and even sometimes the thoughts and conclusions of others I felt were inspiring. These notes are by no means comprehensive.

On several occasions I have been encouraged to write a book about some Bible story or to compile facts for reference. This is my attempt to do so. I will continue to add to these notes as I continue to read, learn and research. This is version one, and it is my hope other versions will come later.

I hope these notes will help you to know more about Jesus. I have spent several years trying to understand Him, and place Him in any particular place and event. I want to synchronize his life through the gospels and history.

Jesus is God in a human body. His footsteps are worthy of study. His life worthy of emulation. I hope you can find it as fascinating as I do.

The notes are grouped by books. Some have a bullet style quick reference of facts. Following that is my assessment of the book's lasting importance and purpose. Finally if I have any insight to the material of the book, I include that also.

The idea is, you can read for background, cut and paste into sermon material, or just use for personal study.

All I ask is please do not give away my years of study like a pirate. I know it is a simple thing to make copies for your friends. I ask you to be honorable and not give away my lifetime of study.

Thank you for purchasing my simple effort to help people better understand the King of Kings and his marvelous book.

Kenneth Bow

Ten Commandments

400 years of slavery had ended with the glorious exodus and the crossing of the red sea. Now the challenge was a new fledging nation with an inexperienced leader contending with a crowd of several million unhappy people.

In a wilderness like desert, without water or food, Moses had to lead several million people to the Promised Land. The task was enormous. God provided Moses with his greatest need, the need of government for this rabble. Moses left to go up the mountain for 40 days, and when he returned, he had in his hand the foundation for every western civilization from that moment forward.

Every nation in western civilization has based their government on the Ten Commandments. It is the basis of the law for all people in the west for the last 3500 years.

How much has the Ten Commandments influenced western civilization? It is, and has been, the bedrock of every single government, whether monarchy, democracy, or theocracy.

The Ten Commandments represent the two great relationships in man's world. First, they represent the relationship man has toward God. This is in commandments 1-4. Secondly, they represent man's relationship toward his fellow man. This would be in commandments 5-10.

The first four commandments are about man toward God. Thou shalt have no other Gods, Not take His name in vain, not make a graven image, and keep the Sabbath. These are about how man is to interact toward his God.

The second six commandments are all about how to exist with our fellow man. Thou shalt not steal, kill, commit adultery, lie, bear false witness, or covet. Each of these commandments helps us survive with others and provide the concept of personal ownership.

This second division is the basis for virtually every law on the books in the United States.

Jesus himself provided this division for us. When challenged by the Pharisees, which was the first and greatest commandment, Jesus gave this reply. He told them that the first and greatest was "Hear O Israel the Lord our God is one." He then said the second is like unto it; thou shalt love thy neighbor as thyself.

To love God and to love our fellow man is the basis for the Ten Commandments. It provides the foundation for all man's relationships.

The Devil knows how important these Ten

Commandments are, so he is trying desperately to remove them from American society at any cost.

Our founding fathers knew their value, so they etched them in stone on the Supreme Court building in our nation's capital.

May the church ever be vigilant to defend the Ten Commandments. When these Ten Commandments perish, the foundation of America will erode and all will be lost.

God help us to love and protect the Ten Commandments.

The Prophets

When Israel left Egypt on that fateful night of the Exodus, they were ill equipped to be a world member in the family of nations. Their centuries of slavery had left them without the basic skills to form a nation and function.

They needed laws and leadership. God provided them with both.

While they made the transition from slavery to a warrior nation to conquer the Promised Land, they needed something to anchor them to their past, to their beliefs and their survival. God gave them the Tabernacle as that anchor. It was the central element that polarized them as a people. It was the central purpose and function of their lives.

The Tabernacle eventually became the Temple and the Temple stood as their foundation and polarization for centuries. The central point and purpose of their lives.

After their conquest and several hundred years of judges and monarchy, they had become an urban people with need of a different anchor. The nation had not become or remained what God had intended. They needed another anchor for a different environment of urban life.

God sent them their second anchor...the Prophets.

The first prophets were miracle workers. Elijah and Elisha types. They got the attention of the Nation at locals like Carmel when Elijah confronted the prophets of Baal.

When it was evident that the miracles alone would not turn the nation back to God, God then sent them a whole new group of men. **The writing prophets**.

About 40 years after Elisha, the first writing prophet appears on the national scene. God introduced the second anchor for the nation. **His word**. From the moment the writing prophets arrived, all of history changed.

These prophets were diverse. Some were highborn, educated and mixed with the highest echelons of society. They were consults of Kings. They were advisors of the highest decisions made in the world.

Others were simple countrymen. They were ridiculed and scorned. Their verbiage and illustrations were simple and homespun. They preached messages, wrote poems, composed songs, and condemned Kings. They are without equal or comparison in any period of history or in any culture in the world.

The Eastern religions for all their lasting impact have never produced the likes of the writing prophets.

The Prophets wrote their visions and conversations with the Almighty. They left behind a glimpse into the mind and nature of God that became the mantle of all preachers for all time. We would not have survived without their writings. Simple or complicated, rich or poor, heard or rejected, to a man, they were magnificent.

Major Prophets

The prophets were God's final answer to disobedient mankind in the Old Testament. God had tried the time of the Judges for 450 years. God then gave the Kings 450 years. The result of both of these was abject failure. Finally he chose to speak to the people directly through the Prophets. When Elijah broke on the scene, nothing was ever the same again.

Elijah the Tishbite came from obscurity and spoke to wicked Ahab and Jezebel, as well as to backslid Israel. Elijah was a new breed unlike anything Israel had ever seen. Elijah and the first prophets were miracle workers. They soon proved about as effective as did the miracles of Jesus. Both these miracle working prophets, and Jesus, teach us there is no lasting value in the miracle as a tool for instruction. Man forgets too quickly.

God then shifted His anointing to the writing prophets. This proved to be the salvation of Israel and eventually the New Testament church. The written word has proven to be the anchor of people for millenniums.

The Major Prophets were not only writing prophets, but preachers to the nation as well. They preached. They cajoled. They begged. They threatened. They pleaded. They did bizarre things to get the people's attention. All to no avail, so they wrote and we are enriched and blessed because of their writings.

There were 16 writing prophets that we have record of. They are responsible for 17 books of the Old Testament. Out of these 16 men, 4 of them are considered Major Prophets. These four are Isaiah, Jeremiah, Ezekiel and Daniel.

A number of reasons have been suggested as to why these qualify as a Major Prophet. What defines a Major Prophet? Some ideas are the length of the writing. But that would eliminate Daniel. Another suggestion is the length of time they spoke, but that would include Hosea who spoke all his life.

I am going to give my assessment as to why they are considered Major Prophets above and beyond the length of their book and the duration of their ministry. Each of the four Major Prophets left a lasting contribution that transcended the centuries and still affect us today on the other side of the New Testament church.

Many of the messages of the Minor Prophets have served their primary purpose and only remain for secondary or tertiary fulfillment. But the final contribution of each of the Major Prophets is still present and being fulfilled. Their contribution was major in the consequences of God's people.

These are my conclusions as to their lasting contributions. These thoughts are expanded in the individual notes on each prophet.

Isaiah: This prophet gives us the concept of the coming Messiah. This is what kept the Jewish people hopeful all through the centuries. They kept believing all through the final crumbling days of the monarchy, through the captivity, during the repatriation, and finally through the 400 silent years. All through this time they were able to cling to the hope, Messiah is coming. When the New Testament opens they are still clinging to this hope. In fact, we still hold to the same hope of the coming of the Lord. This is Isaiah's lasting contribution that elevates him to the status of Major Prophet.

Jeremiah: Jeremiah gives the greatest Old Testament concept of all. Into the heart of a fourteen-year-old boy God flowed 1000 years of history, failure, and disappointment. From the heart of this young man, chosen from his mother's womb and set apart for ministry, came the New Covenant. God said I wrote the law on tables of stone and man has never realized his potential. Now I will write them on the tables of human hearts. That is the contribution that elevates Jeremiah to Major Prophet status. Jesus built his ministry on this concept. Paul built his theology on the covenant given to us by Jeremiah.

Ezekiel: Ezekiel gives us the concept that the glory of God that resides in the heavens, is coming to earth. His book opens with the glory of God in a bizarre vision. Then the last few chapters of his book show the glory of God coming to this earth. He has visions of the temple, the river, the bones, and the two sticks. Ezekiel's lasting contribution is he reaches up into the heavens and pulls the Glory of God down to this earth. That concept elevates him to Major Prophet status, and gives hope and faith to this very day. Jesus is coming and he will bring His glory to this earth.

Daniel: Daniel does not need much by way of explanation. He gives us the entire worldview until the end of time. His writings gave God's people comfort that the roll call of time was still on track century after century. No matter how bleak the day or season, they were comforted by Daniel's writings, everything was right on time according to God's plan. This far reaching, and comprehensive timeline elevates Daniel to the status of Major Prophet.

Minor Prophets

All of the issues that produced the Major Prophets are the same for the coming of the Minor Prophets. They are called "minor" for several reasons in my opinion.

First of all they are generally very brief in length. Next, they are generally narrow in their application and audience. For example, the Major Prophets spoke to the nations around them as well as to Israel. Minor prophets focus on one area or nation.

Next their subject material is focused on a limited time era. They generally are not dealing with a broad period of time. And lastly, it is my opinion many of them played a supporting role to the Major Prophets. Many of them were contemporaries with the Major Prophets.

They also, like the Major Prophets are diverse in background and ministry. One thing is startlingly clear; God dealt with a world, not just Israel. What an amazing revelation to all the Bible scholars who insist God was exclusively interested in the nation of Israel. Some of these men of God spoke solely to Gentile nations. There is the example of Jonah and Nahum to Nineveh, and Obadiah and to Edom.

A poor analogy is: these men were short stories compared to the novels the Major Prophets wrote. They are short, concise diatribes to very particular audiences. They played an important role in the moment of their existence, but did not have the distilled major contribution that the Major Prophets had.

The Minor Prophets are God speaking a brief conversation with Israel, while the Major Prophets were a long involved discourse for many years.

However, do not let yourself think for even a moment they are less in importance. To take that opinion would strip from you their magnificent contribution to God's overall plan. The Bible was written by Holy Men of God, and the spirit of God included each of these "minor" books for a reason that God saw need for.

The pageantry and principals in these books span from the Assyrian empire to the end of the Old Testament under the Persian Empire.

In the Hebrew writings these twelve books were one book called the book of the twelve. There were actually twenty-one segments broken at different places without stopping at the books beginnings.

If read as one continuous book like the Hebrews do, it is quite a journey. You will visit palaces and market places. You will go from world capitals to country dells and villages. You will read of Kings and harlots, siege and famine, plagues and songs of victory. You will read of war and envy, of conquest and human endurance.

Above the din of this cacophony of human existence, you will hear the voice of a loving God, desperately in love with His people. It is the voice of God weeping, wooing, and willing His people to return to Him.

The key to your automobile may seem small and easily replaced, but without it you aren't going anywhere. God saw they were needed and served a purpose, and we would be incomplete without them.

When studying one of these small brief conversations with God, I suggest you remember that the Creator saw the need for this to complete the Book of the ages. Words from God called men, brief and pointed, that are forever settled in Heaven.

Could not all of us take encouragement from this, knowing that God included us in His master plan? No matter how large or small our part on the grand stage of time, we are still important. Without our part, the whole would be lacking. While it is true that taking Obadiah out of the Bible would not have the same effect as removing Isaiah, it was God who decided Obadiah needed to be in the book that is forever settled in heaven.

It is apparent that God placed value on each man who contributed to the Bible. What a lesson. Will any of us refuse to do our part because it seems small and less important than that of others?

Her are my thoughts on the Minor Prophets as to who they spoke to and when:

- Hosea, Wrote to Israel the northern kingdom, about 700 BC
- Joel, wrote to northern kingdom about 800 BC
- Amos, spoke to northern kingdom during Jeroboam II reign, 700 BC
- Obadiah, spoke to Edom (Esau's descendants), His date is very controversial
- Jonah, spoke to Nineveh (world empire), 200 years before Nahum
- Micah, spoke to northern kingdom, same time as Isaiah
- Nahum, second voice to Nineveh
- Habakkuk, spoke only to God, his book is a Theodicy, after the captivity
- Zephaniah, spoke to the repatriated nation, after the captivity
- Haggai, same as Zephaniah, spoke to the nation after the captivity
- Zechariah, spoke to the nation after captivity and rebuilding of the temple
- Malachi, spoke to the repatriates at the close of the Old Testament

One of my most helpful thoughts has been to think of about ten ministers you know. Think of how they preach. Think of how they approach a subject. Think about their vocabulary, their illustrations, and their message. That will give you a good appreciation of the Minor Prophets and their diversity.

They were courageous men who devoted their life to delivering God's message. It was almost universal that their message was unwanted and unheard. Yet, they obeyed their call and completed their message.

I look forward to the day when I can sit and talk with them and learn the rest of their story.

They were a magnificent breed indeed.

The Monarchy

God called a nomad named Abram around 1900 BC and began a nation. From his loins came Isaac, then Jacob, then the twelve tribes and eventually the Hebrew nation. From there the 70 souls went down to Egypt to escape the famine and emerged some 400 years later to cross the Red sea and do the wilderness journey.

Once they entered the land of promise there was a period of time of about 450 years when Judges governed the land. While the nation was making the journey from a nation of slaves to a nation of farmers the Judges worked well enough. Then slowly they began to emerge as a nation of cities and a whole new need arose.

Soon the cry for a King like other nations began and finally became a din that God answered. The time had come for Israel to have a king and the monarchy was born. Coming on the heels of the Judges, it certainly looked like anything would be an improvement. Sadly that was not to be.

Before the Monarchy had run it's course it would

eliminate 10 tribes forever and take all 12 tribes to spiritual lows never known before, and to this day, never matched again.

There was the period of the United Kingdom for 120 years. Each of the first three Kings ruled for 40 years (Saul, David and Solomon). Those 120 years was followed by a civil war that resulted in the nation being torn into two nations known thereafter as Israel and Judah.

Israel was the northern kingdom and was comprised of 10 tribes. Over the next 200 years there would be 19 kings in a row and every one of them were bad. Not one King in 200 years of the northern kingdom served God. Finally God had enough. In 721 BC the nation of Assyria came and conquered 46 cities and led away 200,000 captives. The Assyrian army marched to the very gates of Jerusalem, the capital of the southern kingdom, and surrounded the city.

Rabshakeh the Assyrian general informed King Hezekiah of the Southern Kingdom they were next on the list to be taken captive. Rabshakeh mocked Hezekiah and said even if I gave you 2000 horses for war, you could not put riders on them. The southern kingdom was at the mercy of the greatest army in the world.

Hezekiah asked Isaiah the prophet what to do and what followed is one of the most remarkable stories in the history of mankind.

Isaiah told King Hezekiah to not worry about those 185,000 men encamped about the city of Jerusalem.

When the Hebrews awoke the next morning they found out that the Angel of the Lord had gone through the camp of Assyria and killed 185,000 men. It ranks as one of the greatest victories ever, anywhere.

The southern kingdom was spared and lasted another 135 years. There were 19 kings and one queen in the southern kingdom. I say there were 8 good kings. It does depend on what you call good. But from my perspective 8 kings in the south were good.

The book of chronicles which was originally one book, (* see note below), like the book of kings, primarily deals with the good kings of Judah. It has even been referred to as the white washed history because it eliminates things like David's sin with Bathsheba. Chronicles focus is on the monarchy that was good, and the temple. These were the two things that had permanence in Hebrew life.

So was the monarchy, success or failure? There were 41 kings in all and one queen. At best 11 kings might be said to have ruled well. That leaves 30 kings who ruled poorly and one queen who was the wicked monarch of all.

The monarchy ruled for 455 years. It was almost the exact same number of years the judges ruled. My conclusion is that it was a failure just as notable as the Judges. God never intended for man to rule over man. God has always been the right ruler in man's life.

Note: The book of Chronicles and the book of Kings were written in Hebrew, which has no vowels. When translated into English both books were too long and so they were divided into two books.

Kings divides when the divine ministry of the prophets begins with Elijah. Chronicles divides with Solomon who builds the temple. No doubt the translators felt the ministry of the prophets, which would replace the monarchy, and the Temple were the natural points to divide the books.

Judges

The book of Judges opens to us one of the darkest times of man's history. The people of God should have been celebrating victories and conquering a new land. Judges opens the window into the heart of mankind, and the picture is not pretty.

Seven times in the book the statement is made "every man did that which was right in his own eyes." The result of that environment was catastrophic. It further emphasis that there was no King in those days. So every man was left to follow his own decisions.

This period of time lasted 450 years. This period of time was as long as the entire duration of the monarchy. Because there is one book of Judges, and six books of the Kings (Samuel, Kings, Chronicles), it is natural to feel like the Kings were a longer period of time. Both of these time periods were 450 years. Why?

God gave man 450 years to reveal what happens when man does that which is right in his own eyes. The result of that time period is so abhorrent and tragic, we scarce can comprehend it. The last five chapters of Judges are as bad and ugly as any period of history, any place on the Globe. From this experiment and experience we can truly agree with God that it is not in man to direct his steps.

It might help to think of these Judges as freedom fighters. The word Judge to us today speaks of courtrooms and juries. These men, (and one woman), were liberators, fighters, leaders of armies. They are renowned for their military campaigns. The following is a list of Judges and their term of time.

Judge	Enemy
Othniel/40 years	Mesopotamia
Ehud/80 years	Moab, Amon, Amalek
Deborah, Barak/40 years	Caanan
Gideon/40 years	Midian
Abimelech/3 years	
Toah/23 years	
Jair/22 years	
Jeptha/6 years	Ammon
Ibzaim/7 years	
Elon/10 years	
Samson/20 years	Philistines
Eli/40 years	Philistines
Samuel/20 years	Philistines

By my addition there were 111 years of oppression and 339 years of peace for a total of 450 years of the reign of the Judges. This is the same amount of time for the Kings. There was 120 years of the United Kingdom, 200 years of a divided Kingdom with Israel and Judah side by side, and an additional 135 years of Judah.

The conclusion I get is this, God gave man 450 years

of man doing what he thought was right on his own. Then he gave man 450 years where a king ruled over his life. Both time periods ended in abject failure. Opening the door for the prophets and God's voice being the law of man and earth. The only successful government has proved to be when God himself rules over the affairs of men.

In the first 16 chapters of Judges, it is all about God's people being attacked from without. The enemy is from the outside. Then the last five chapters are the result when Israel turns upon herself and begins to carnage herself. The result is one of the most terrible times in all of history. Before it is over Israel will have killed more of her own that any of her attackers from the outside. If fact, she will have killed more of her own that all of the outside attacks combined over the entire 450 year period.

What a statement God leaves on the pages of the Bible about what happens when we forget who our real enemy is and begin to war on our brothers.

In the last five chapters, it begins with the introduction of Idolatry into Israel with the story of Micah and his graven images. The stage is set for idolatry and it takes a thousand years, a dispersion (Israel), and a captivity (Judah), to finally purge Israel of Idolatry.

The story moves on to the tribe of Dan. This tribe is not satisfied with their inheritance so they look for new territory. They journey east, then north, a total of about 144 miles to conquer Laish. They rename the city "Dan"(hence the term from Dan to Beersheba). This is not the inheritance God assigned to the tribe of Dan. This story lets us see the terrible result of what happens when you are not satisfied with your inheritance. The tribe of Dan is forever removed from the pages of the Bible. The only mention I find is one descendant worked on Solomon's temple. Dan is never mentioned again, never included anymore in the list of the tribes all the way to the book of Revelation.

What more would anyone need to illustrate the danger of not being satisfied with our inheritance?

The book of Judges then moves on to the story of the concubine. The woman was abused and finally dies. Her master cuts her into twelve pieces and sends a piece of the evidence to each tribe. The nation goes to war and the result is horrific. Israel loses 65,000 men in the final chapters of Judges, all because they had a piece of the evidence. The tribe of Benjamin is reduced to 400 men and almost obliterated. I believe they would have been wiped out if not for a future son of Benjamin that would literally change the world, Saul of Tarsus. God preserved the tribe for Israel's first king, and Christianity's first missionary.

The moral of the story is again so stark. It is so dangerous to go to war over a piece of the evidence.

Was all lost for humanity? Not at all. God in his infinite wisdom was letting man work through the slow process of human government to help man self-discover for himself his need of God.

All was not lost, for even in this morass, at the bull's eye center of the greatest carnage were faithful people who held on to God. That is why Boaz steps onto the stage. There was in the days of the Judges, Ruth 1.1

We will discuss that in the book of Ruth.

Psalms

God gave mankind the five books of the law and a grateful mankind gave back to God the five books of the Psalms.

- Book 1 chapters 1-41
- Book 2 chapters 42-72
- Book 3 chapters 73-89
- Book 4 chapters 90-106
- Book 5 chapters 107-150

The collators of the Psalms took time to place these books in their current order to correspond with the first five books.

- Book 1 relates to Genesis
- Book 2 relates to Exodus
- Book 3 relates to Leviticus
- Book 4 relates to Numbers
- Book 5 relates to Deuteronomy

God presented mankind with the law and a grateful Israel responded with a Pentateuch of praise in acknowledgment of God's gift. The psalms are a second Pentateuch, the echo of the first. This may be pure conjecture, but the existence of this idea from ancient times shows that the fivefold division attracted early support in history.

Placed in the center of the Bible, rising like a tune from the very heart of the Bible are these songs. These songs wrestle with the deepest sorrow and ask God the hardest questions. These songs cry out to God and at other times shout for pure joy. The God they sing of is not a distant God, but a God that is near and personal.

They span over a thousand years of human circumstances. There is a psalm to match every human emotion and mood. They put your unspoken thoughts into words and form your unspoken conversation toward man and toward God. They give backbone to the raging emotions of humanity.

Psalm 1 and 2 have been called the orphan psalms and are the introduction to the entire body of psalms. God starts out with Blessed (happy) is the man who does not do certain things.

True happiness is not in unbridled liberty, but rather in the restrictions God places in our lives. The more narrow the channel, the more raging the current. No boundaries or limits allow a body of water to be one inch deep and forty miles wide.

Such is our lives. When God's boundaries are observed, our lives are happy and blessed. When those boundaries are ignored or removed, we are a stagnant unhappy people.

The last 5 psalms are the great doxologies of the Temple.

They were written for and sung at the dedication of the repatriated temple. There is not a single syllable of complaint or request in these last psalms. They are pure undistilled praise. Each one begins and ends with "Praise ye the Lord."

The authors:
- David 73 psalms
- Asaph 12 psalms
- Sons of Korah 9 psalms
- Solomon 2 psalms
- Moses 1 psalm
- Roughly one third are anonymous

The psalms were used in the temple daily:
- Monday psalm 48
- Tuesday psalm 82
- Wednesday psalm 94
- Thursday psalm 81
- Friday psalm 93
- Saturday psalm 92
- Sunday psalm 24

The subscriptions and superscriptions above and below the psalms are important. Many people do not even notice them. They add explanation and impact. Here is a list that I have of the titles, subscriptions and superscriptions.

- Aijeleth shahar- the day dawn
- Al Alamoth- relating to maidens (sopranos)
- Al Taschith- destroy not
- Gittith- the winepress (sang at harvest of grapes)
- Higgaion- a soliloquy or meditation
- Jeduthun- name of one of the 3 chief musicians

- Jonath Elim Rechokim- the dove in the far off Terebinth trees
- Mahalath- the great dance
- Mahalath leannoth- the great dancing and shouting
- Maschil- understanding or teaching psalm
- Michtam- engraving, permanent writing
- Muth Labben- death of a champion
- Neginoth- smitings (like smiting a string on an instrument to bring forth music)
- Nehiloth- the great inheritance
- Psalm
- Selah- pause like a musical rest, can mean, "What do you think of that?"
- Sheminith- the eighth
- Shiggaion- loud passionate cry, emotional outburst
- Shoshannim- lilies, re: Passover feast

To understand the psalm adds greater meaning. Example, when David sinned with Bathsheba he repented and said he would teach transgressors God's ways. Psalm 32 is the psalm David wrote for that purpose. It is a maschil psalm, a teaching psalm, to teach the transgressor how to get back to God.

Putting words to music somehow imbeds them deeper into our memory. Like a child learning the ABC song, these psalms were sung to drive the lesson deep into the learner's mind.

How important are the psalms? When dying on the cross, Jesus quotes from the psalms. (22.1,31.5). In the disciple's efforts to explain Jesus' life, they quote the psalms more than any other book or part of the Bible.

On a personal note, I believe the 119th psalm was written by Daniel. There is much speculation about this. Some attribute it to Hezekiah. My reason is the writer makes no mention of the temple, or the ritual law. The writer has powerful enemies who could do him harm. He is a young man. He is in love with the word. That picture speaks to me of someone in a foreign land without the formal religion to lean on. The word was all he had, so that became the love of his life. That speaks to me of Daniel.

May the Bible become that to each of us on our life journey.

Song of Solomon

Love stories have captured the hearts of men and women since the dawn of time. Lovers are forever linked together, even centuries after their lives are over. The names of Romeo and Juliet, Marc Antony and Cleopatra, Dante and Beatrice, Hosea and Gomer, live on even now, eternally linked together.

The Song of Solomon is a love story. It may very well be the greatest love story ever told. Solomon was named by God Himself as the wisest man who ever lived. He knew as much about women as any man ever has. He had 700 wives and 300 concubines. I think that qualifies him for nomination for a PhD in womanology.

Solomon wrote three books. He wrote the Song of Solomon as a young man. He then wrote Proverbs when in middle age. Later when he was elderly, he wrote Ecclesiastes.

He, who wrote 1005 songs and 3000 proverbs, said this was the Song of Songs. Out of the 1005 songs he wrote, this was number 1. Is it feasible that he wrote a song for each of the women in his life? Possibly

1000 women and 1005 songs. We know this song was written to the Shunamite girl and we know she resisted his enticements. So, I suggest it is at least possible his modis operandi was a love song to each woman he courted.

Out of all the songs he wrote, he felt this was the Song of Songs. The question is why? I submit it was because he saw in this young girl the kind of love he wished Israel as a nation had for God. If somehow Israel would fall in love with her Shepherd like the Shunamite girl loved her Shepherd, then Israel would be blessed.

The story goes something like this. Solomon had a summer home. This we find in the Bible. While making the journey there one summer day he sees a young shepherdess and a young Shepherd under an apple tree.

That night Solomon sends for the young girl who is black by the sun and very poor. She has never had nice things or even shoes upon her feet. When she is brought to Solomon's palace she is overwhelmed. When Solomon makes his intentions known, she is speechless and is given until tomorrow to make up her mind.

There are 140 women with Solomon at this time. While she lies upon her bed with her head spinning, she hears the young Shepherd boy at her door. He has come looking for her. He is panicked at the thought of losing her to Solomon. He has braved the dangerous night to find her and take her home.

While lying on her bed, she hesitates and he moves on. Finally she rises and goes to the door, and can smell his lingering fragrance. She runs through the night city looking for him but he has gone.

The next day when she appears before Solomon, he makes his plea for her. She is torn between the pull of Solomon and all he can offer and her Shepherd lover. Solomon makes a fatal mistake when he mentions the apple tree. When Solomon says that her mouth is like apples, she rises and flees. She runs from the summer palace and runs home.

The Shepherd is disconsolate because he thinks she is lost to him. Then suddenly he sees her. She is running to him. Her garments are flying in the wind. Her hair is blowing free. The Shepherd realizes she loves him more than all the allurements of money or fame. The time spent under the apple tree with him forged a bond between them that was as strong as death. She is reunited with her Shepherd lover.

Back at the summer palace, the whole court of Solomon is aghast. The young girl just ran out. No one had ever done that before. They were stunned. They were stunned because the girl had the nerve to reject the King, but even more stunned by the King himself.

He just sat on his throne with a puzzled look on his face. For a long time he said nothing. Then he asked for a writing instrument and something to write on. They were amazed. Why, he was writing a song. A song of tribute to the woman who could not be bought. To the woman who was so in love with her Shepherd, that nothing could influence her to give that love up for another love.

Slowly they began to see what the King saw. If only God's people would love their Shepherd that way. Solomon hummed the tune to The Lord is my Shepherd. For the first time in his young life, Solomon understood true love. A love based on time spent together. A love that was not based on things, but rather on value of each other.

The wisest man of all the ages wrote a song about that and declared it to be the "Song of Songs." A tribute to the love for a Shepherd that was forged under the Apple tree. A love so strong that even death itself could not sever it.

May God give us that kind of love for our Shepherd.

Isaiah

It he eighth century BC while Homer was writing the Iliad and the Odyssey, and Lao Tse was writing the Tao de Ching, Isaiah wrote the book that bears his name.

The prophet Isaiah was a giant of Jewish history. He is considered the Shakespeare of Hebrew literature. The New Testament quotes him more than all the other prophets added together. No author in the Bible can match his eloquence and mastery of style and imagery.

He lived midway through the founding of the nation and its final destruction. He lived on the border between the Northern and Southern kingdom. He was one of the prophets who observed first-hand the fall and captivity of the Northern Kingdom of Israel.

The Rabbis say that he was first cousin to King Uzziah. Isaiah's father, and Uzziah's father, were brothers. This would mean he was of royal lineage, and familiar with the palace and court life. He certainly was the confidant and advisor to at least 5 kings.

Isaiah was not a "yes" man to these kings. He stood against the popular tide of optimism. His name meant

"The Lord saves." He warned Kings repeatedly that to depend on military power or wealth or alliances or anything but God would bring disaster.

Isaiah outlived four of the kings he advised, but finally offended one King beyond the King's tolerance. Manasseh is said to have placed Isaiah between two planks and had him sawed in half. Thus ending the life of one of Israel's greatest heroes.

Isaiah's writings are about the nature of God. It is a collection of many messages on many subjects.

His writings break down like this:

- Chapters 1-12 warnings to Judah during their prosperous days
- Chapters 13-23 messages to surrounding nations
- Chapters 24-35 earth's future and the imminent invasion of Assyria
- Chapters 36-39 an interlude telling of crisis Judah faced
- Chapters 40-48 prophesies 200 years into the future (Babylon)
- Chapters 49-55 The nation's final deliverance through the suffering servant
- Chapters 56-66 warnings to Judah and a view of the future

These are quick bullet references to Isaiah:

- Began preaching before he was 20 years old
- A contemporary of Amos and Hosea
- Born during Uzziah's reign
- Called in the year Uzziah died

- Saw the Glory of Jeroboam II (Israel)
- Observed the fall of Israel in 721 BC
- Influenced Hezekiah
- Foretold the rise of Babylon
- Killed by Manasseh
- His book a mini Bible (66 chapter, 39,27)
- Proclaims the coming Messiah
- Quoted more in New Testament than all other prophets combined
- Shakespeare of Hebrew literature
- First cousin to Uzziah
- Giant of Jewish history
- Lived exactly in the middle of the founding of the nation and it's destruction
- His name means "the Lord saves"
- Prophesied during 5 kings
- Wrote same time as Iliad, Odyssey and Tao de Ching
- Looks into the nature of God
- He was Hezekiah's "song in the night"

His supreme contribution was his fore telling Messiah is coming. The nation hung onto this thread of hope until Jesus arrived. It helped keep them through the 400 silent years of despair. When the New Testament opens they are on point looking for Messiah.

Because he looks into the nature of God, He is our "One God" preacher. Verses like, 9.6, 7.14, 43.10-11, 44.6, 44.8, 45.15, as well as chapters 12, 35, and 53, are favorite one God passages. When an Apostolic preacher preaches on Oneness, he invariably visits the book of Isaiah.

When Assyria threatened the nation, after conquering

200 walled cities and leading away 200,000 captives from the northern nation, it was Isaiah who stayed calm while Hezekiah panicked. Isaiah was the song in the night with a word from the Lord. The next morning 185,000 Assyrians lay dead, Judah was saved, and Isaiah was right.

Isaiah had heard from God and the Angel of the Lord went through the camp of Assyria and slew 185,000 men while Israel slept and never lifted a finger.

The Devil was not alone in using Giants to do great exploits. God answered with some Giants of his own.

Of these, none stands taller than Isaiah.

Jeremiah

Which fourteen-year-old boy in your church can you envision preaching and being God's Mouthpiece? That was the age Jeremiah began his prophetic work. He then proceeded to speak to a nation who would not listen for the next 40 years.

He has been called the "weeping prophet" because of the times in his book he sheds tears. Jeremiah prophesied while his nation tottered on the brink of captivity.

Jeremiah certainly lived one of the most dramatic lives in the Bible. It appears he never learned to like his role. He was reluctant and unhappy with the job God asked him to do.

God chose him before he was even born, while he was still in his mother's womb. His assignment was to be over nations, to root out, to tear down, to build and to plant. The only resource he had to accomplish this task was his mouth. His response? "Ah Lord God, I cannot speak, for I am a child" (1.6)

He was given the unusual directive that he could never marry; never attend a happy event or a sad event. He was not to experience any human emotion so he would never be confused as to what he felt. He felt what God felt.

For forty years Jeremiah gave the nation's leaders messages they did not want to hear. They arrested him, they imprisoned him, and they almost killed him. Jeremiah hung on. He let them know that the Babylonians were coming and would carry them into captivity. He warned them that alliances with powers, like Egypt, would not do any good. They ignored him and he pressed on anyway. Jeremiah made it clear, Judah's only hope was to renew their relationship with the living God.

Jeremiah does not impress us like Isaiah. His book is not poetic or beautiful in imagery. The power of the book comes entirely from the insight of this prophet's mind. He was living a nightmare and that nightmare was coming true. The nation was going under.

No person in the Bible shows their feelings like Jeremiah. He quarreled with God. He told God he wished he were dead. He accused God of being unreliable. And yet, he stood, never wavering. No relationship in the Bible speaks more to me of what it means to serve God. He continued to follow God no matter what.

I am sure he tired of the ridicule. He continued to stand alone against the crowd. He spoke dark things in dark times. His message was not wanted or popular. In the end his message proved true. He stands greater and more important to the kingdom of God than the very Kings who detested him.

The book of Jeremiah is an anthology of prophecies given at different times. It jumps back and forth and is not in any chronological order. It is a glimpse into the troubled mind of a man trying to warn a drowning nation.

300 years before the nation had been split into two nations with the civil war. Israel and Judah had existed side by side for 200 years. Then, 100 years before, the northern nation had been carried away into captivity into Assyria never to be heard from again. He was seeing deja vu for Judah. This time mighty Babylon was breathing down their neck and invasion was imminent.

Bullet points for Jeremiah:

- Prophesied during 5 kings
- Lived through the Babylonian invasion
- Contemporaries were Zephaniah and Habakkuk
- He was forbidden to marry
- He was forbidden to go to any social meetings, happy or sad
- His book has no particular order
- He was called at 14 years old and preached for 40 years
- Tradition says he was stoned in Egypt at the end of his life
- He was the first person to speak of 70 years, then Daniel picked it up
- Never liked his role but he obeyed
- His only weapon was his voice
- He was one man against a surging mass going in the opposite direction
- He quarreled with God and told God he wished he were dead (20.14-18)

- Accused God of being unreliable (15.18)
- Had no social life (16.8)

Some of his memorable messages:

- Broken cisterns
- Potters house (18)
- Rechabites (35)
- The miry clay
- The buried sash
- The smashed pot
- Purchasing land for the return after the exile

His supreme contribution:

It is my opinion that Jeremiah gives us the high point of the Old Testament. In chapter 31 he gives the turning point after 1000 years of failure as a nation.

God wrote the law on tables of stone and the nation never was able to fulfill their destiny. It was smoke, ashes, debris, and failure. It was time for the second edition to be written.

Abraham was called in 1921 BC. The children of Israel entered Canaan in 1451 BC. It had been 1300 years since Abraham's call and 800 years since they crossed the Jordan. The judges, the kings, the prophets, had all proved unable to stem to tide.

God called a fourteen-year-old boy. God quarantined him from social events, and gave him the New Covenant. 1000 years of history flowed into this young boy's heart. From that river flowed out the New Covenant that is the foundation of the New Testament.

This time God would write it not on tables of stone, but on their hearts. Jeremiah chapter 31 becomes the foundation of all the teachings of Jesus and the Apostle Paul.

It is an incredible story of an incredible man, used by God.

Ezekiel

Like the prophet Jeremiah, Ezekiel was a priest as well as a prophet. Ezekiel was carried away captive in 597 BC by Nebuchadnezzar's army. He was taken to Telabib on the river Chebar.

He was married and had his own house (chapter 8.1). His wife died on the day Jerusalem was taken and he was told by God to not mourn or show sorrow (2 Kings 25.1, Ez 24.1, 15-18).

He began to prophesy in the 5th year of captivity and had 13 visions and prophecies that are dated. For the first 6 years he prophesied to the captives while Jerusalem was still standing.

One of his jobs was to keep the sins of the people that had caused the captivity, to be in their thoughts. 70 times Ezekiel says, "They shall know that I am God." 7 times he says, "The hand of the Lord was upon me."

Ezekiel's book has three divisions:
1. Jerusalem before the siege
2. After the fall of Jerusalem, to the 7 nations around Judah
3. Future glory of God's people

He uses visions, signs, parables, poems, and proverbs in his prophesies.

He is called son of man 100 times.

It appears to me that he preaches 10 messages in the first 24 chapters without speaking at all. He remains dumb. He lies on his side, uses a tile, uses a razor, uses a pot, and uses fire, to illustrate his sermons.

It is my opinion that he uses these methods to reach the younger generation. The older people had already proven that they would not listen. It appears to me that God was reaching for the younger generation, who would in 60 years return to the Promised Land and rebuild the temple.

Ezekiel uses these dramatic sermons to try and make them messages to be remembered.

Because he is a contemporary of Jeremiah, they are known as the stereo prophets. Jeremiah stayed in Jerusalem and prophesied while Ezekiel prophesied in Babylon.

Ezekiel's lasting contribution is concerning God's glory. When his book opens he sees the glory in the heavens. It is Ezekiel's wheel in the middle of the wheel. By the end of his book, that glory has been brought down to earth, and the entire world sees God's glory.

Ezekiel's prophesies about the two sticks, the valley of dry bones, the river to swim in and the temple, all these things speak of God's glory coming to earth.

One thing is for certain. Jesus is coming, and when he comes, He will bring his glory and fill this earth with holiness unto the Lord.

That promise is Ezekiel's lasting contribution.

Daniel

Daniel is considered a major prophet, even though his book is not that lengthy. In my notes about the Major Prophets I explain that it is more than length that determines a major prophet.

Daniel was carried away captive into Babylon in the first wave of captivity. There were three waves of captivity. In the first wave Nebuchadnezzar carried away the finest young men and minds of Jerusalem. He then carried away 10,000 and placed them in a captives settlement on the River Chebar. Ezekiel was in this group. Then the final gleaning carried all the rest into Babylon in 586 BC (2 Kings 24).

Daniel probably would have had a great career in Jerusalem, but he was never given the chance. At 18 years old he is ripped from his prominent family and carried away into a faraway country. The Babylonians did not care about his dreams or plans. He was a refugee to them, a captive.

The Babylonians saw his potential and trained him in their schools. After his graduation Daniel was put to work for the King. This same king Daniel worked for, continued to war against Daniel's people for another 20 years.

I find no record of any family members around Daniel. It appears he was alone except for some other young men also carried captive.

Daniel rose to the position of Prime Minister. For an outsider to achieve this high position speaks volumes about Daniel. He kept this position for many years, even when Kings were dethroned. Daniel's career at the top lasted at least 66 years. When he was thrown into the Lion's den he was over 80 years old. There is no finer example in the Bible about how to live and excel with people who do not serve your God or share your beliefs.

Later in His life, God gave Daniel a series of visions about the future of planet earth. In graphic terms God showed Daniel the future. Daniel's people would duplicate his personal experience on a world scale. God used Daniel to show the Hebrew people what to do when the Diaspora unfolded.

The Hebrew people thought they had exclusive rights to God. The book of Daniel shows God's intent was to save the world, not just the Jew.

To me one of the most magnificent things the book of Daniel offers, is the proclamations by heathen kings. These proclamations brought more honor to God than anything a Jewish King had done in decades. Daniel's book teaches how God's people can live caught in the jaws of brutal world politics.

Daniel continues his career at least until the 3rd year of

Cyrus. Cyrus was a despot. When Cyrus was killed, the queen cast his head into a vat of blood and said, "Thy thirst was blood, now drink thy fill." Somehow this incredible man Daniel was able to navigate all these treacherous waters of politics, and remain unscathed.

The first 6 chapters of his book are stories about the life in Babylon. The rest of his book is a series of visions about the world's future.

An interesting note is that before the captivity is final, Daniel refers to God as "Lord of hosts." After the captivity happens, he refers to God as "The God of heaven." I wonder if he felt God had moved out of planet earth because of the captivity?

When Nebuchadnezzar conquered Jerusalem, he carried away 2499 vessels. These were kept in storage until Cyrus gave the permission to return and rebuild the Temple. Then these vessels were used in the rebuilt temple.

I am of the opinion that it was Daniel that signed the decree to rebuild Jerusalem. That decree was issued in the first year of Cyrus, and Daniel continued at least until the third year of Cyrus. What an honor to live your life in such a manner to be the one to attach your signature to the rebuilding of the temple.

I am also of the opinion that Daniel is the author of Psalm 119. This great Psalm sings of the word of God. That was all Daniel had. Whoever wrote Psalm 119 had no temple to attend. The author had enemies in high places, and was persecuted for his love of God. These parameters seem to fit Daniel perfectly. If this is true, how it must have thrilled him to be able to sign the document to rebuild the temple for all future Jews.

Daniel had had to live for over 80 years without the house of God, but future generations would be blessed again with a temple. His exemplary life allowed him to see this come to pass.

In addition to his long and fruitful career in foreign palaces, he also had a personal audience with the archangel Gabriel. He also took up Jeremiah's theme of 70 years and gave us the 70 weeks of years.

How much more magnificent could one life be? Finally let me offer this about Daniel.

Daniel speaks about how a young person can do great things for God. He was a contemporary of Ezekiel. It is simply amazing to me how Daniel receives honor from his peers. In Ezekiel 14.14, Ezekiel says though Noah, Job and Daniel stood before me, they would deliver but their own souls. Again in chapter 28 and verse 3, Ezekiel speaks of the wisdom of Daniel.

For future generations to venerate you and speak of your greatness is not that uncommon. Here is a young man while in his prime that is seen by his peers as one of the greatest of all time. Ezekiel looked at Daniel and placed him with Noah and Job, then used Daniel as the ultimate measure of wisdom.

Show me another example in the Bible of a young man who gathered that kind of honor while still young. Show me another young man in the Bible who received such honor from his peers, and from God himself.

Daniel was a giant of his day. Daniel is still one of the truly great men of the Bible. The shadow he casts reaches across thousands of years.

Inter-testament Period

They are called the 400 silent years. Interesting that the whole world was convulsing with worldwide change, yet Biblically it was silent. While the world heard marching armies and battle cries, heaven was mute toward earth. It is called silent because there is no recorded instance of God speaking to man during this time.

When Malachi laid down his writing instrument, there was not a voice from God until the days of John the Baptist. When that stern Essene, John, lifted his voice for the first time to preach, 400 years of silence was shattered. How heaven must have rejoiced. God was again on speaking terms with His creation.

You are reading your Bible. You finish the Old Testament. You turn the page. You continue to read, not thinking of the vast time and change that happened in the turn of that page.

Because we are familiar with the New Testament, we do not stumble at terms like Pharisee, scribe or synagogue. But none of those, nor many other terms, are used in the Old Testament. Were you not familiar with the Bible, you would indeed be scratching your head saying what is a Hasmonean? What is a Herodian? These and many other important Bible subjects and issues emerged during this silent period.

When the Old Testament closes, The Babylonian Empire has fallen and the Media Persian Empire has taken over. Cyrus the Persian has allowed the decree to rebuild the temple in Jerusalem. The Old Testament prophets have died, and there is a huge spiritual vacuum.

The writings of Daniel chart the course during these silent years and let Israel know all is on track as God predicted. Without Daniel, would they have been able to persevere? We do not know.

From the standpoint of world history, how do we measure the importance of the Greek Macedonian empire? The leader of Greece at this time was Alexander the Great. He is called "the Great" for some valid reasons. The cities the Greeks built, and the culture they exported to their conquered lands (Hellenism), was world changing. Romans built upon the foundation Greece had laid.

This period of Greece was followed by the Roman Empire, which lasted 700 years and had two Pax Romanas (empire wide peace). Rome built the roads that missionaries would travel. Rome brought peace so missionaries could travel in relative safety. Yet all of Rome and Greece's Hellenestic influence is unmentioned or never referred to by God. Heaven's record and evaluation appears to be far different than mortal men.

When Paul begins his missionary journeys that would transform the known world, these issues of Hellenism would play a major part. God placed these issues in the mosaic of time for all to be fulfilled when the fullness of time came to pass.

Cyrus the Persian was tolerant and allowed the repatriates to return to the land of Israel. According to Ezra only 42,000 or so elected to return. Babylon had been good to the Jewish merchants and life was plush. They had no desire to endure the rigors of the journey back to Palestine. Then after they arrived they would be required to live more primitive and frugal. The majority said "no thank you."

Their needs had changed as a nation. Idolatry, that had been the albatross around the national neck for a thousand years, had finally been put away during the captivity. The death of idolatry, as strong as idolatry had been, was final. To this day none of us know of a single instance of a Jewish person who worships idols.

The Jewish people needed guidance. Into this vacuum stepped the scribe. Ezra was the forerunner of this elite group so highly esteemed. They were to play a vital role in Jesus' day.

In captivity they had no temple to worship at, so the Synagogue was established. Any place ten Jewish males lived the Rabbi's decreed a synagogue was to be built. The Rabbi was the local leader of the synagogue. Some Rabbis became famous and venerated among the population.

Here are some terms that play a part in the New

Testament that are not in the Old Testament, but are there when you turn that page from Malachi to Matthew.

- Scribe (mentioned in Ezra)
- Synagogue
- Pharisee
- Sadducee
- Hasmonian
- Herodian
- Essene (non biblical term)
- Sanhedrin
- Governor (Roman)
- Tax collector
- Zealot

All of these are important in the inter-testament period.

These are my definitions of them.

Scribe: Became the leaders of the community. Interpreted the law for the common man.

Synagogue: House of worship for Jewish people all over the world. Visited every Sabbath.

Pharisee: Keepers of the law. Very concerned with detail. Jesus' main opposition for three years. Not powerful in the government, for they could not get Jesus arrested.

Sadducee: Wealthy group as a whole, many of them members of the Sanhedrin. Did not believe in the resurrection. When Jesus raised Lazarus from the dead and offended them, Jesus was arrested and put on trial.

Hasmonian: These were the Jews who wanted to merge with the Greeks and the Romans. They were ashamed of their Jewish heritage. They dressed like the Greeks and Romans. They even went so far as to reverse circumcision, so when they went nude in public like the Greeks, no one would know they were Jewish.

Herodians; These were a political group loyal to the Romans and the line of Herod who were puppet kings installed by Rome

Essenes: These were people who lived apart in communities like communes. They ate, dressed and lived very sparingly. John the Baptist was an example of an Essene.

Sanhedrin: This was a Jewish council allowed by the Romans to adjudicate Jewish laws. Rome did not want to deal with the petty issues of a conquered nation's differences. This group was comprised mostly of Sadducees, and consequently wealthy men. History says the number was 70 who were on this council. Maybe they chose the number from Moses' day?

Governor: When Herod the great died he divided his kingdom into three parts. He gave one of the parts to Archalaus his son who was extremely vial. The night Archalaus inherited, he killed 3000 Jews to entertain his guests. Rome removed him for his cruelty and replaced him with a governor. There were several governors before the New Testament opens, but at Jesus' trial the governor was named Pontius Pilate.

Tax collector: The Roman Empire lasted 700 years.

American has lasted about 250 years. It is easy to see Rome was around a long time. Their success in part was due to how they adjudicated the subjugated peoples they conquered. As a rule they left the national laws and traditions in place and this contributed to their longevity as an empire. They followed this policy with Palestine. All Rome asked was the tax due the empire. So they leased out the collecting of taxes to the highest bidder. The tax collector kept whatever he could extort from the people. As a rule the tax collectors were despised as rouges and crooks. Matthew, Jesus' disciple was a tax collector.

Zealot: Maybe a more familiar term to us would be revolutionary. A zealot was a person who wanted to over throw the Roman power over Palestine. One of Jesus' disciples was a zealot, lending credibility to the charges against Jesus that ultimately got Him crucified.

To the world at large the 400 years were not silent. It was business as usual. There was commerce and war, peace and revolution. There was the siren song of time marching steadily forward.

Finally after 400 years of heaven's silence, in a far-flung corner of the mighty Roman Empire, a child was born and a son was given. Heaven has never been silent since, and will never again hold its peace.

God was manifest.

The Talmud

I suppose at first thought, you might wonder why a note on the Talmud, when many other books of the Bible are not included yet. There are a couple of reasons.

First, I wanted to include some things that give support and understanding on how God views our journey here on earth.

Secondly, I wanted to include the note on the Talmud because it supports our position on holiness in this present day.

The Torah is the Jewish name for the Pentateuch. The Pentateuch is the first five books of the Bible. The Talmud is the collection of commentary from Jewish Rabbis on the Torah.

Why would this be important to us as Gentiles? My answer is it provides such a beautiful example of how to survive in a world that does not understand us as Apostolics. To live in our world, which views us as outdated and eccentric, is becoming more difficult as society drifts farther and farther from the principals of the Bible.

The Jew has survived in every century, in every culture, and in every continent. The Jewish life is as strong today as it was 2000 years ago. As Apostolics, we need to adopt some of the same principles to insure we do not lose our identity.

The five books of Moses can be written out in about 350 pages. The Talmud now takes up 523 books in 22 volumes. As the Jew was scuttled from empire to empire, the need arose for a protection from the blows without and the pressure from within. The Talmud has provided that. The Talmud has become the home of the Jew no matter where he lives in the world. The Talmud has single handedly provided the survival of the Jewish person.

As Apostolics, it appears to me that we are in danger of losing our heritage of holiness. More and more I see whole churches assimilated into our worlds culture and mores. We need holiness and separation more than ever before.

The way we dress and live must not die with this generation. As simple as it may seem, our standards are what will keep us separated from the world. Simple things like sleeve length, and the distinction of dress between male and female, are critical to the survival of the Apostolic heritage. It provides us with the cold concrete of protection from the blows that come from without.

In the Talmud, there are many issues that may seem insignificant. But upon inspection the Talmud provided the Jew with answers to the baffling questions of life. The Talmud has done more to preserve the Jewish way of life than any other factor.

This oral law that has been discussed over the centuries has kept the Jewish people uniquely Jewish. It is my hope that our holiness standards will keep us Apostolic in a world that has lost all sense of direction.

The Rabbis have haggled over every phase of Jewish life. They have argued over every word and comma. In the process of mulling all this over, they created a mandate for survival in a hostile world.

When the world attacked, the Talmud was there to soften the blow and stiffen the will. Other ancient cultures have faded from the earth, but the Jew has survived. Can we learn a lesson from them?

The authors of the Talmud seemed to think that no issue was too small to discuss. They would debate for months whether a person could wear a false tooth on the Sabbath. A tailor could not take his needle in his hand just before the Sabbath because he might forget and go out with it. You could have candy in your mouth as long as it was put in your mouth before the Sabbath began.

They discussed for nine years one statement in the law; "Thou shalt not seethe a kid in his mother's milk." From this one issue came the whole idea of Kosher food and food that was not Kosher.

Our first response might be, that is foolish and insignificant. But never forget it is the small things that have kept them as a people. They have survived.

We need to appreciate the "small" things if we are going to preserve this Apostolic way of life. Our standards of dress are important to our survival. Our standards of what we watch and what entertainment we allow is important to our future. Our survival depends on the small things.

I will be the first to admit that the Rabbis went to extremes to preserve the Jewish way of life. However, it is beyond argument that the Jew has survived while other people have been assimilated and have vanished from the stage of time.

Our survival as a distinct people depends on the small things. We must maintain our holiness and our standards of life.

When they become unimportant, you can write the epitaph of the Apostolic movement.

Jesus

His names are many. The Messiah, Son of Man, Son of David, King of Israel, Savior, Servant, The Prophet, Son of God, and the Christ. He was hailed and acclaimed as the being who held the highest spiritual status attainable in human form. The perfect one, the Avatar, God as man.

To some he was nothing more than an extraordinarily wise and compassionate teacher. To others he was a political revolutionary who had divinity projected upon him by his followers. To some he is just a myth, a legend; he never really existed at all.

No figure in history has provoked so much controversy and debate, nor inspired so much faith, as Jesus. Today the religion based on His teachings called Christianity, is the largest religion in the world. 1 billion, 900 hundred million, on every continent, in almost every country.

The Mexican peasant in his hovel claims to be a Christian. The Cardinal in Rome, in rich robes and elegant rings, claims to be a Christian. The African learning English in a missionary school, is a Christian.

The New York businessman signing papers in his office 30 floors above Wall Street, is a Christian.

Christianity has spread across the globe touching every culture and society on earth. Christians believe that Jesus is the Son of God. He was sent to earth to save humanity from their ignorance, suffering, and sin.

What we know about Jesus comes almost exclusively from the gospels. Jesus left no writings, so the gospels are the primary source of information about His life.

Matthew and John knew Jesus and followed Him. Luke and Mark received their information from others.

There are all kinds of debate among scholars. Some say none of these men ever really knew Jesus and did not even use their real names. They question everything; they are skeptics.

In the time Jesus lived, there was a strong oral tradition of passing information from generation to generation. This oral tradition was an art form. People carefully memorized the information. They worked hard at retaining the original facts and flavor. This oral method of preserving information was how Homer's Iliad and Odyssey were preserved. It is more reliable than our modern journalism. Some prodigies memorized up to a million words by the time they were 12 years of age.

The earliest information written on Jesus that does not come from His followers comes several years after His death. There are remarks by Josephus, who wrote around 90 AD. Pliney the younger wrote about 112 AD, Tacitus wrote around 115 AD, and Seutonius wrote around 120 AD.

When you combine all these, Christian and non-Christian, we get a basic outline of Jesus life. There are large gaps in Jesus' life we have no information on. We do know of His birth in Bethlehem. His birth was probably around 6BC, when Herod the great was King. There is a brief glimpse when Jesus is 12, then nothing more until He becomes an adult.

Historians do not agree on the day Jesus was born. The best conclusion is September. This was John the Baptist father's week in the temple. There were twenty-six weeks by the priesthood, where they served only twice a year. So John was born in March or September, Jesus comes six months later. We know He was crucified in the spring and His ministry was three and a half years, so September is the only possibility. We do not know the day.

The December 25th date is of pagan origin and was adopted 400 years later to appease the pagans of the Feast of Saturnalia.

Jesus was born in Palestine. It had always been a troubled area, bathed in blood. This area was shuttled back and forth between world powers, Assyria, Babylon, Greece, Antioch Epiphanies, and Rome. In 63 BC Pompey the Roman General captured Jerusalem. The Romans allowed the Jews to retain their religion, and a figure head king (Herod). Then the Romans simply appointed a Governor to rule over Judea after Herod Archelaus was removed because of his cruelty.

Pompey was defeated in 63 BC, by Julius Caesar. Caesar was assassinated in 44 BC. Mark Antony came briefly to power, and then Octavian replaced Mark Antony.

Through all of this Herod and his line maneuvered and kept the title "King of the Jews." The Romans mocked, and smiled indulgently at this absurdity.

After Herod massacred the infants, Herod's son, Archelaus, took the throne. The night his father Herod the Great died, Herod Archelaus became tetrarch of Judea, Idumea and Samaria. Another son Antipas was given Galilee and Perea. Phillip became tetrarch of Trachonitis, Iturea, Batanea and Auranitis. Caesar approved this.

Remember… Joseph and Mary had to flee to Egypt to escape Herod the Great, but when Herod Antipas imprisoned John the Baptist, Jesus simply left because Herod Antipas had authority only in Galilee.

These Herods were wicked men. Archelaus inaugurated his reign the night his father died, carousing with friends, and slaughtered 3000 Jews in the Temple. The Jews appealed to Caesar and Archelaus was banished. So Judea was free of Herods.

Caesar said, okay I'll appoint a ruler, so he appointed Quirinius Caponius, then Ambivius, Annius Rufus, Valerius Gratus, then Pontius Pilate. Pilate ruled from 26-36 AD. Pilate was so cruel Rome removed him 3-6 years after the Crucifixion. It was his cruelty that led to his dismissal.

The Romans divided the area into Judea (with

Jerusalem) and Galilee. In the New Testament, Judea was governed by Pilate; Galilee was governed by Herod's family. (This is the reason Pilate sent Jesus to Herod; Herod was the puppet king of Galilee).

The people of Palestine suffered terribly under both the Romans and the Herods.

****

If you look for Him, you will see Him…

In Genesis, Exodus, Leviticus, Numbers Jesus is there. He was there in every chapter and every line. You will see Him in the coats of skin that cover Adam and Eve's sin. You will see Jesus in the blood of Able that speaks of better things.

You will see Jesus in Moses' face, sent to deliver his people out of Egypt. You will see

Jesus in the blood on the doorpost and lintel.

If you look for Him, you'll see Him in the meal offering, for He is the bread of life.

You'll see Him in the wave offering for He was offered up for our sins.

You'll see Him in the drink offering, for He was poured out so I could be saved.

You'll see Him in the feast of weeks and feast of the tabernacle. He is my tabernacle, my outer court, my inner court, and my holiest of holies.

He is my meal offering, my drink offering, my bread, and my incense.

He is the door by which, if any man shall enter in, he shall find green pastures.

He is the candlestick that lights my way into the presence of God.

He is my light, my bread, His blood is my wine, and He is the veil; for when the Roman soldier pierced His side, the veil was rent in twain.

The rending of His flesh gives me access to the Father. I have stepped behind the veil into the holiest of holies, because of Jesus.

Don't look down your nose at me if I get excited when I praise Him. He is my "all in all," my everything.

He is Aaron's rod that budded, my high priest, my pot of manna, He is my ark of the testimony, He is my fulfilled law, He is my Sabbath, for when I am in Him I find rest and peace. I cease from my labors and find rest. "Come unto me all ye that labor… I will give you rest." Somebody praise Him.

He is my Shekinah glory; He is my glory of God. He lights my dungeon.

He is my cloud by day pillar of fire by night, my brazen serpent in the wilderness – I had been bitten by sin, but He was lifted up and I am healed.

He is my tree that was thrown into the bitter waters

of Mara, He changed my bitter life into sweet water, and He is my rock, smitten on Calvary, whose gushing waters quench the thirsting of my life.

****

The Incomparable Christ

He came from the bosom of the Father to the bosom of a woman. He put on humanity that we might put on divinity. He became the Son of man that we might become the sons of God.

He left the region where the rivers never freeze, winds never blow, frosts never bites, flowers never fade; where no doctors are needed, because no is ever sick; where graveyards never haunt, death never comes, where no funerals are ever conducted.

He was born contrary to the laws of nature, lived in poverty and reared in obscurity; only once did He ever cross the boundaries of His own small country.

He had no wealth, training, or education, and whose parents knew nothing of the niceties of social tradition.

In infancy He startled a king; in boyhood He puzzled the wise; in manhood He ruled the course of nature.

He healed the multitudes without medicine and made no charge for His services.

He never wrote a book; yet all the libraries of the world could not contain all the books that could be written about Him.

He never wrote a song, and yet He has provided the themes for more songs than all earthly writers combined.

He never founded a college, yet all the schools of earth have not had the students that sat at His feet.

He never practiced medicine, yet has healed more broken hearts than the world has ever taken note of.

He never marched an army, never drafted a soldier, or fired a gun, yet no leader has ever had the volunteers who under His orders, made rebels stack arms and surrender at His command, never firing a shot.

He is the Star of astronomy, the Rock of geology, the Lamb and Lion of zoology, the Harmonizer of all discord, and Healer of all diseases.

Great men have come and gone; He lives on.

Herod could not kill Him; Satan could not seduce Him, death could not destroy Him and the grave could not hold Him.

He laid aside His purple robe for a peasant's gown. He was rich, but for our sakes became poor, that we might be rich.

How poor?

Ask Mary. Ask the wise men.

He slept in another's manger; He rode another's beast; He was buried in another's tomb.

All others have failed; He never.

The ever perfect one: the Chief among ten thousand; altogether lovely:

THE INCOMPARABLE CHRIST

****

Jesus… there's something about that Name.

In Genesis… He is the Creator…sun, moons, stars, worlds, man, animals, flora & fauna, cosmos, universes infinitive.
In Exodus… He is our Passover Lamb
In Leviticus… Our Law Giver
In Numbers…Our Brazen Serpent, high and lifted up
In Deuteronomy…Our "Hear O Israel, the Lord thy God is One"
In Joshua…Captain of the Lords Host
In Judges…Our Faithful Judge
In Ruth…Our Heavenly Kinsman
I & II Samuel…Our King in the midst of Blessings
I & II Kings…Our King in the midst of Apostasy
I & II Chronicles…Our Restorer of a lost nation
Ezra…Our Faithful Scribe
Nehemiah…Our re-builder of broken down walls
Esther…Our Mordecai
Job…He's the one who believes in us when our Friends flake out.
Psalms…Our song in every circumstance on life's road
Proverbs…Our answer to life's riddle
Ecclesiastes…Our wisdom
Song of Solomon…Our Shepherd in the night.

Isaiah…The Son, Immanuel, Wonderful, Counselor, Mighty God, our Everlasting Father, and our Prince of Peace
Jeremiah…Our weeping prophet
Lamentations…The Eulogy of a fallen nation
Ezekiel…The four faced man in life's trial
Daniel…The fourth man in life's fiery trial
Hosea…Our Rapah, our Husband, our Redeemer.
Joel…The Holy Ghost Giver.
Amos…The Shepherd who gathers the broken pieces of our life and heals us.
Obadiah…The recompense to our enemies
Jonah…Our evangelist
Micah…Our light in the darkness
Nahum…Our judgment on unrighteousness
Habakkuk…Reviver of our work in the midst of our years
Zephaniah…The Re-gather of a lost nation
Haggai…Fruit Giver to a starving & barren nation
Zechariah…The Olive Tree and the Candlestick
Malachi…The echoing voice of God that reverberated for 400 years.

Matthew…Son of Abraham
Mark…Son of Man
Luke…Son of God
John…The Word which is; which was and which is to come.
Acts…The Holy Ghost
Romans…Our Justifier
I & II Corinthians…Our Sanctifier
Galatians…The breaker of the curse of the law
Ephesians…He who repairs our broken down wall of partition that kept us from God

Philippians…The Name at which every knee shall bow
Colossians…All the fullness of the Godhead bodily
I & II Thess…Our coming King
I & II Timothy…God manifest in the flesh
Titus…Our washing of regeneration
Philemon…Our deliverer from slavery
Hebrews…High Priest and our New Covenant
James…Our Faith that makes devils tremble
I & II Peter…He quiets the scoffers of all ages
I & II John…Our Love, or propitiation
Jude…Our contender for the faith that was once delivered to His saints
Revelation…Our Alpha, our Omega, our First and Last, our King, our Priest, our Lion our Lamb, our Savior, our coming King, our Judge, our redeemer, and The Almighty

Jesus, there is something about that name.

Matthew

The Bible is the best-selling book of all time. Therefore it is reasonable that the Bible is the most read book of all time. Statistics say that Matthew is the most read book of the Bible for almost everyone starts there.

Now if you or I were going to write a book that we knew more people were going to read more than any other book in the history of the world, would we start it out with a long list of names that no one can even pronounce? Yet God in His wisdom does just that. Why?

Well, one supposition is that He loved the Jewish nation and preferred them with the first Gospel in honor to His commitment to them through the centuries. One thing is for sure; Jesus was not the Messiah they were looking for. He did not fit the image of their expectations.

The Jewish nation was looking for someone to come in and overthrow the Roman grip on their land. Jesus came to overthrow the grip Satan had on their land. So we have the Gospel of Matthew…

- Matthew was a tax collector, therefore he speaks of money more than any other writer, (example, Peter go catch fish and there will be a coin in its mouth)
- He starts his genealogy with Abraham instead of Adam because his book is to the Jew
- He has 31 passages unique to him, 10 parables, 2 miracles, 9 discourses, 6 events
- He is the only gospel writer to mention the church
- Uses the term Kingdom of Heaven because the Jews did not use the name "God"
- Writes like a tax collector, Example 8 beatitudes at start of book and 8 woes at end, like bookends
- His style is narrative, discourse. Jesus' story then, speech or sermon. 5 times says "when Jesus had ended these sayings"
- Quotes the Old testament more times than any other New Testament writer (129 times)
- 16 times says "that it might be fulfilled"
- 2 great sermons, sermon on the mount, and Olivet discourse

There had been 400 years of silence. Then Matthew's gospel pulls it all together. It is the bridge. Matthew portrays Jesus as the King of the Jews. His gospel is considered as the most important book in Christendom by the French skeptic Renan.

One of the great contributions of Matthew to oneness people is his information on the transfiguration. In chapter 16 Matthew begins the story of Jesus leaving the area of Galilee and going north to the regions of Caesarea Philippi. Jesus literally turns His back on the country of Israel and goes to a gentile region and spends about 8 days with His disciples.

After 6 days of rest and relaxation, He poses the question to them, who do men say that I am? It is a supreme moment in Jesus' earthly journey. For 3 ½ years He has prepared this select group of men for this revelation. They offer the current scuttlebutt of names, and then Simon Peter makes the famous reply, "Thou art the Christ."

Jesus no doubt breathed a sigh of relief knowing they had truly got the concept of His being the messiah. Two days later is a remarkable event. I call this "When a good Jewish son took over the family business."

The event is called the mount of transfiguration. Jesus waits another 2 days and then takes Peter, James, and John with Him up on the mountain. Matthew, Mark, and Luke all inform us what happened there.

Jesus is transfigured before them and Moses and Elijah appear with Jesus. The disciples are speechless, and stunned. Peter finally blurts out an inane babbling, something about three temples.

These three disciples are witness to the transfer of all spiritual spokesman ship from the Father to the Son. A voice booms from the heavens and says, "This is my beloved son, in whom I am well pleased; hear ye him."

This same voice had spoken at the baptism of Jesus, but had not said, "Hear ye him." At that moment, the eternal spirit of God proclaimed His residence forever to be in the man Christ Jesus. Christ's earthly ministry was complete. The only thing left was to be the perfect sacrifice.

Never since that moment has the voice of God ever spoken outside of Jesus Christ. The voice that spoke worlds into existence, the voice that spoke to Moses on Mt. Sinai, now speaks only through the mouth of Jesus Christ. He is God manifest in the flesh.

Go to your Bible and look. God has never spoken again outside the mouth of Jesus Christ. What a wonderful revelation to the oneness of God. Truly in him dwelleth all the fullness of the Godhead bodily.

Mark

Mark's gospel was the first gospel written in 50 AD. It was written to the Roman world. It came at a very critical time. The Caesars were killing the Christians in Rome and there was fear and consternation across the empire. Nero was on a rampage. The need was for direction. And the need was now.

So we have the Gospel of Mark. It is the shortest Gospel because time was of the essence. It is the fastest paced Gospel. It uses hurry up adverbs 42 times. Words like immediately, and straightway are the norm.

I am convinced Mark's Gospel was dictated by Simon Peter. This was a commonly held belief well into the second century. Papias says this in AD 60-150. Papias call Mark Peter's interpreter. Probably Peter spoke in Aramic and Mark translated into Greek. Finally, Peter calls Mark his "son," 1 Peter 5.13.

Mark is the timeline that Matthew and Luke work off of. 90% of his gospel is found in Matthew and Luke. He is fast. He has three miracles in the first chapter. The other writers wait until chapter three before introducing a miracle.

Because it is to the Roman world, Mark quotes the Old Testament only one time. He ignores the Mosaic Law, and then explains the Jewish laws and the Passover. Once again, time was pressing them to get this message into the hands of suffering Christians.

It is the shortest gospel, and is proclaimed by an eyewitness, so hence the nod goes to Peter. Matthew repeats over 90% of Mark in his gospel and Luke repeats over 53%, (330 out of 660 verses).

It is interesting to me that Mark does not mention anything about Jesus before Jesus' baptism. No birth, no early years, or any other information.

Also, Mark deals with Jesus' humanity. Mark shows Jesus tired, weary and hungry. The Roman world and the new Christians needed to be reminded He was the Messiah. The Avatar, the highest form of God in humanity.

In all probability, the Christians of that day expected the return of Christ any day. They no doubt saw no need for a record of his life, for they would all remember. However when He did not return quickly, it became obvious a whole new generation needed the facts to be recorded.

It is certainly reasonable to assume that Mark knew all the early church leaders and populace. He was a relative of Barnabas and traveled with Barnabas and Paul on their one and only missionary journey together.

Mark is also believed to be one of the few men who accompanied Simon Peter to Cornelius house in Acts chapter ten.

Luke

The third Gospel is the only one written by a Gentile. Luke also wrote the book of Acts. His two works comprise 25% of the New Testament.

Luke was a doctor. The flavor of the man always comes out in his writings. In Luke we see more conversation about women, Gentiles, and the social outcasts. When a beggar lays at the gate of the rich man, Luke says he was full of sores. Matthew would have said he was broke. Matthew's perspective as a tax collector was his financial status, while Luke had the perspective of a doctor.

Luke's gospel is written to the Greek, or Gentile world. He uses Mark as his time line and repeats somewhere around 50% (320 of 661 verses), of the same material Mark provides.

Because he is writing to the Gentile world he begins his genealogy at Adam. Matthew goes back to Abraham, Mark bypasses the genealogy, and Luke goes back to the first man Adam. John, who writes to the church, reaches back to the misty darkness of eternity.

It appears to me that Luke took the time to interview the people of the early church. He states that his book is from the beginning and that he had perfect understanding of it all.

When you read of Jesus' birth in Luke's account, you find some tidbits of information no one else includes. One example would be the details of Mary's song and inner thoughts and feelings.

That causes me to think Luke must have sat down with Mary and spent time talking to her. I can envision him sitting quietly many years later, at the end of her life, recording her words as she softly speaks of those bygone years. As she wistfully remembers, he dutifully records.

Not only does he provide information about people's feelings and inner thoughts, he also documents his writings with names, offices and titles of over 50 people. This gives his work a credibility the other gospel writers do not have to the world of scholars.

One example of his documentation is the introduction of John the Baptist in chapter 3. Luke places 7 men in the scripture for historical evidence. He mentions an emperor, a governor, three tetrarchs, and two high priests. These are the kind of things that give Luke credibility with the world of scholars. This also gives further credibility by association to the other Gospels who give the same information. For this alone Luke is invaluable.

Another contribution of his is the writing of parables spoken by Jesus. He records 18 parables not recorded anywhere else. We are indebted to him for the famous parable of the Good Samaritan, the prodigal son, and many others.

I am going to go out on a limb here and state my opinion for what it is worth. I know that Luke traveled with Paul. I am somewhat sure he joined Paul on one of his missionary journeys, because the text of Acts changes from they, to the first person of I and we. So my thought is that somewhere Luke sat and listened to Paul tell his insight into the life of Jesus. My best guess would be this occurred while Paul was being held at Caesarea.

Just like when he started his book by making the journey to see Mary, I can see Luke taking notes at the feet of Paul and then the Holy spirit washing them though the man Luke with his training, his education, and his perspective. From out of that flowed the gospel of Luke.

The gospel written to the Greeks adopts the Greek idea of the perfect man. The Greeks created their Gods by deifying man into a God.

Luke very ably and perfectly adopts their premise and presents them with the perfect man, who was indeed God, Jesus Christ the savior of the world.

John

John was Jesus' first cousin and His best friend for 3 ½ years. Jesus' mother and John's mother were sisters. No man on earth knew the story of Jesus better than John. His gospel is a magnificent treatise to the life of Christ and its impact on planet earth.

His gospel is different than the others. Very different. It is written like John is sitting under a shade tree with his feet propped up, just daydreaming about the life of Jesus. He only selects vignettes, short insights or events, from 20 days in the life of Christ.

John uses the simplest words, and a small vocabulary to plunge us into the deepest mysteries of God. John uses the vocabulary of a six-year-old child. A child learns about 100 words a year and John uses about 600 words in his writing.

The words John selects are powerful words. He uses words like world, father, light, and truth. He uses the simplest words to paint a profound God and His plan.

Matthew writes to the Jew, so he begins his gospel at the lineage of Abraham. Luke writes to the gentile Roman world, so his lineage begins at Adam. John writes to the church, so he reaches all the way back to eternity. He begins with, "In the beginning."

John reaches back to the inky blackness of eternity, before there was the brush of an angel's wing. He reaches back before there was the first blazing shaft of light that shattered the darkness. When there was nothing but God. In the beginning was the logos, the word, the thought, the intent. And the logos was God.

John does not cover the same material as the other three gospels do. The only miracle he repeats is the feeding of the 5000. He writes to the church about 60 years after the other writers. The church was facing many challenges.

When John wrote, there were those who said Jesus never really existed. There were others saying Jesus was not a human, but rather a phantom. Other views at that time proclaimed Jesus did exist but he was just a man with divinity projected upon him by his disciples. It was into this morass that John wrote his gospel.

John writes of no parables, and uses 7 signs to build his story of Jesus. He explains things like no other writer. When he tells a miracle, he often explains why he used that miracle. An example would be the feeding of the 5000. He tells us Jesus is the bread of life. The other three writers did not explain the connection for us. When Jesus heals the blind man, John explains Jesus is the light of the world. It is his explanations that give his gospel an added dimension.

He also includes things of immense importance. Consider how important John chapter three is to the doctrine of the new birth. The story of Nicodemas is the bedrock of salvation. Ye must be born again. That one inclusion validates the day of Pentecost and the doctrine of the New Testament church. Chapter by chapter, John gives the church a gospel for the ages. He delivers the most profound insight into Jesus the man, of any writer of history.

2/3 of John's book is about the last week of Jesus' life. Fully 1/3 of his book is about the last 24 hours of Jesus' earthly life. After 60 years, the need was for a complete record of the importance of Calvary. A whole generation had arrived that were not eye witnesses to the events of Jesus' death. Someone needed to write it down and John succeeded as Heaven's emissary.

We have the gospel of John and it is indeed magnificent.

Acts

Oft times I have wondered about certain books of the Bible. I have thought, what if we did not have this book in our Bible? How would that affect the whole? When I place the book of Acts on that pedestal, and consider, I am certain of the answer.

Only Acts and Genesis seem to hold the place of absolute. Without them we simply could not survive. They are both irreplaceable.

The book of Acts was written by Luke. Luke is the only Gentile writer in the Bible. It is interesting to me that Luke is responsible for 25% of the New Testament. His two books equal one fourth of the volume of the New Testament.

I am not positive, but it appears to me that Luke wrote at the bequest of a wealthy patron named Theopholis. His two books address this individual. This was a common practice that carried well into the middle ages. A wealthy patron would sponsor someone to write a book or thesis. This is how men like Voltaire and Rousseau were supported financially.

To me, Acts is about three men. Those men are Simon

(Peter), Saul (Paul), and Stephen. The book is evenly devoted to the ministry of Peter and Paul with Stephen being the bridge from one to the other.

The contrast of these two men is stark. Peter is a country fisherman. Paul is a polished cosmopolitan. Peter was ignorant and unlearned. Paul was a trained rabbi, having studied at the feet of Gamaliel. Peter spoke Aramaic, the common language. Paul could speak that language, as well as Greek. Peter was a country Jew; Paul was a Hellenistic Jew and a Roman Citizen.

The first twelve chapters of Acts are about Peter. In chapter 13 the spotlight shifts to Paul and never moves back to Peter again. Peter, the great apostle fades from view in Acts.

How important is Acts as a book? It is irreplaceable! Without the book of Acts we would go from the Gospels to Romans. We would wonder who is Paul? What is the church? How did it start? Acts is the link to all of the New Testament.

Acts begins with the ascension of Jesus. It moves on to choosing Judas' replacement. It then tells of Pentecost, the beginning of the church, and eventually documents the church's emigration to the Roman Empire.

Christianity conquered the Roman Empire, period. The Roman Empire paved roads, established peace and continuity, and through this open door walked the church. The church flourished during the Pax Romana, the empire wide peace. Within 300 years 10% of the Roman Empire was Christian.

The book of Acts documents the beginning of this conquest of the church.

When the spotlight shifts to Paul in chapter 13, Luke begins to relate Paul' missionary journeys. Paul made three journeys. (Some scholars say up to five). The dates of these journeys are:

- 46-48, first journey
- 49-52, second journey
- 53-57, third journey

It is simply amazing that in 47AD there were no churches in Asia Minor. In ten years there was a ring of churches that included every major city in Galatia, Macedonia, Asia and Acacia. This remarkable achievement has never been repeated anywhere globally.

On his first journey, when he gains his first convert, the Apostle Paul jettisons his Hebrew name Saul, and forever becomes known as Paul. He was the Apostle to the Gentiles and he bore his Gentile name to his death.

Luke is a gentile, writing a book about the gentile revival by the Apostle to the gentiles. This fact shows up in the book repeatedly. It is very clear in the story of the appointment of the deacons. When the division came and the controversy showed itself, out of the seven men chosen, 5 were Greeks according to their names. Luke makes this point, or rather the Holy Ghost does.

The final chapters of the book of Acts are concerning

Paul's last days. I am left with one of the biggest questions of my life as to why the book ends so inconclusively. With the Holy Ghost inspiring the man called Luke, why no closure?

My only hypothesis is that the book is still being written in heaven. Maybe the final words were something like "to be continued."

What chapter will you write to add to the book of Acts?

www.ingramcontent.com/pod-product-compliance
Lightning Source LLC
Chambersburg PA
CBHW040325300426
44112CB00021B/2883